THE PROBLEM WITH EARLY CLOCKS

BLOOPERS OF INVENTION

OOPS!

BY RYAN NAGELHOUT

Gareth Stevens
PUBLISHING

Please visit our website, www.garethstevens.com. For a free color catalog of all our high-quality books, call toll free 1-800-542-2595 or fax 1-877-542-2596.

Library of Congress Cataloging-in-Publication Data

Nagelhout, Ryan.
The problem with early clocks / by Ryan Nagelhout.
p. cm. — (Bloopers of invention)
Includes index.
ISBN 978-1-4824-2768-4 (pbk.)
ISBN 978-1-4824-2769-1 (6 pack)
ISBN 978-1-4824-2770-7 (library binding)
1. Clocks and watches — History — Juvenile literature. I. Nagelhout, Ryan. II. Title.
TS542.5 N34 2016
681.1'13—d23

First Edition

Published in 2016 by
Gareth Stevens Publishing
111 East 14th Street, Suite 349
New York, NY 10003

Designer: Sarah Liddell
Editor: Ryan Nagelhout

Photo credits: Cover, p. 1 Jonathan Kantor/Stone/Getty Images; p. 5 DEA/G. CIGOLINI/Contributor/ De Agostini/Getty Images; p. 7 (Roman calendar) Leemage/Contributor/Universal Images Group/ Getty Images; p. 7 (Mayan calendar) Vadim Petrakov/Shutterstock.com; p. 9 (main) Three Lions/ Stringer/Hulton Archive/Getty Images; p. 9 (sun clock) Dorling Kindersley/Getty Images; p. 11 Dmitri Kessel/Contributor/The LIFE Picture Collection/Getty Images; p. 13 (candle clock) Heliocrono/Wikimedia Commons; pp. 13 (main), 15 (main) Print Collector/Contributor/Hulton Archive/ Getty Images; p. 15 (pendulum clock) Science & Society PIcture Library/Contributor/SSPL/ Getty Images; p. 17 (main) Zbynek Jirousek/Shutterstock.com; p. 17 (inset) Matt Cardy/Stringer/ Getty Images News/Getty Images; p. 19 (diagram) Encyclopaedia Britannica/Contributor/Universal Images Group/Getty Images; p. 19 (quartz watch) turtix/Shutterstock.com; p. 21 SCIENCE SOURCE/ Science Source/Getty Images.

Printed in the United States of America

CPSIA compliance information: Batch #CS15GS: For further information contact Gareth Stevens, New York, New York at 1-800-542-25onathan

CONTENTS

Words in the glossary appear in **bold** type the first time they are used in the text.

TELLING TIME

Do you know what time it is? Maybe you're wearing a watch on your wrist or there's a clock on the wall. Being able to tell time is important. Maybe you have to go to bed at a certain time or need to make sure you don't miss your favorite show on TV.

Most clocks we use today are **mechanical**, but what about a clock that uses the sun or water to tell time? Let's check out all the wacky ways people have told time throughout history.

OOPs!

Metrology is the science of measurement. Clocks are used to measure time. If you measure it wrong, you'll never know what time it really is!

THIS IS AN EXAMPLE OF WHAT THE INSIDE OF A MECHANICAL CLOCK LOOKS LIKE.

USING THE SKY

One early method of telling time was using a calendar, not a clock. Ancient people—such as Sumerians living in Iraq, Syria, and Iran more than 5,000 years ago—used the moon to track time. Their calendar had 30 days in a month, and each day had 12 periods that lasted 2 modern hours.

The Mayans, living in Central America between 2600 BC and AD 1500, made a 260-day and a 365-day calendar using the moon, the sun, and the planet Venus.

OOPS!

One cycle of the Mayan calendar ended on December 21, 2012. Some thought that meant the world was going to end!

ancient Roman calendar

Mayan calendar

THE 12 PERIODS OF A SUMERIAN DAY WERE BROKEN DOWN INTO 30 DIFFERENT PARTS, WHICH EACH EQUALED 4 MINUTES OF OUR TIME.

SUN CLOCKS

Ancient Egyptians used the sun to tell time. They built obelisks, which are tall, four-sided towers that get narrower as they rise. As the sun rose and set, the obelisk created a shadow on the ground that moved. Putting marks on the ground around the obelisk that matched the shadows, the Egyptians could tell what time of day it was. This is also called a sundial.

Egyptians also made a sun clock, which was portable, or could be moved. It measured shadows with a raised **crosspiece** at one end.

OOPS!

Sun clocks need shadows to work. If it's nighttime or it's cloudy out, you can't tell what time it is!

EGYPTIANS MADE THE FIRST
SUN CLOCK AROUND 3500 BC.

obelisk

sun clock

WATER WORKS

Water clocks were one way people measured time without using the sun. One of the oldest water clocks made was found buried with an Egyptian king. **Archaeologists** think it was made around 1500 BC.

A common kind of water clock was made from two bowls. One bowl sat above the other, and **gravity** helped the water flow out. Some had markings on the higher bowl that showed how much water had flowed out. Others had marks in the lower bowl to show how much water had flowed in.

OOPS!

It's very hard to control the flow of water, which meant water clocks weren't as **accurate** as other, later clocks.

GREEKS CALLED WATER CLOCKS "CLEPSYDRAS," WHICH IS GREEK FOR "WATER THIEVES."

11

GREAT CANDLES

Alfred the Great is sometimes credited with inventing the candle clock. Alfred was a king in England from AD 871 to AD 899. He kept time with six candles that burned for 4 hours each.

Alfred used the candles to keep track of how much time he spent on eating, sleeping, praying, studying, and kingly duties. Adding a weight, like a nail, to a candle clock meant it could be used as an alarm. When the candle burned through, the weight fell and made a noise!

OOPs!

Early candles had wicks that didn't burn away. They had to be cut off, or the heat from the burned wick could melt the wax and set the alarm off early!

candle clock

THE CANDLE CLOCK WASN'T ACTUALLY INVENTED BY ALFRED THE GREAT. USING A CANDLE TO TELL TIME WAS MENTIONED IN CHINESE WRITING DATING BACK TO AD 520.

13

WEIGHT FOR IT

Christiaan Huygens, a Dutch scientist, made a pendulum clock in 1656. A pendulum is a weight that swings back and forth at the end of a pole. The length of time each swing takes depends on how long the pendulum is. A pendulum's motion moves other weights or springs. They make the hands on a clockface move.

On a clockface, the short hand tracks hours and the long hand tracks minutes. Early weighted clocks became less accurate as their springs got stretched out. They would need to be wound again.

OOPS!

The early weighted clocks that hung on walls were so heavy they fell and broke. Finally, pendulum clocks were put in cases standing on the ground.

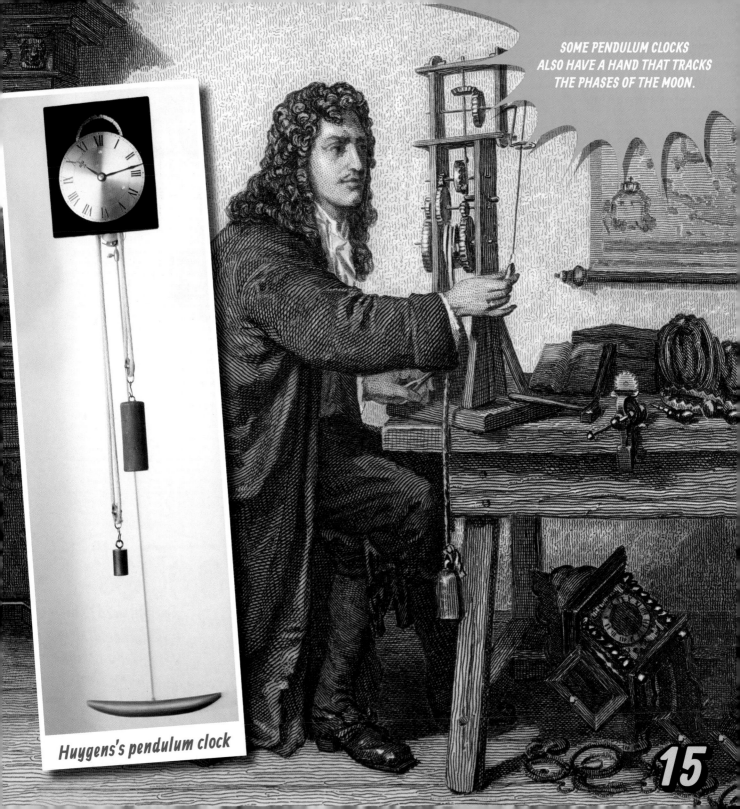

SOME PENDULUM CLOCKS ALSO HAVE A HAND THAT TRACKS THE PHASES OF THE MOON.

Huygens's pendulum clock

15

WHEELS IN ACTION

Mechanical clocks became more accurate with the help of moving gears called a wheelwork. People would wind the clock, which powered the wheelwork and moved the clock's hands.

The large main wheel connects to a smaller one that in turn connects to smaller and smaller gears. One gear rotates, or spins, once per hour to track hours. A smaller gear tracks minutes, rotating once per 60 seconds. Other gears track other things, but all the parts work together smoothly.

OOPS!

Many clocks still need to be wound to keep time accurately. You can often hear a ticking clock and see if it is moving too fast or too slow.

world's oldest mechanical clock

USING CRYSTALS

In the 1920s, clocks started using a crystal called quartz. Quartz is used as an **oscillator**, which keeps the clock moving at a certain rate. This made quartz watches and clocks more accurate.

Electricity is sent through the crystal and used to power the clock itself. Quartz watches are only off about 1 second every 10 years! Most quartz used in watches today is synthetic, or man-made. It's made watches cheaper to make.

OOPS!

Quartz watches often get their energy from a battery. You need a new battery when it runs out of energy or the watch stops working.

QUARTZ IS ONE OF THE MOST COMMONLY FOUND MINERALS ON EARTH. A MINERAL IS MATTER IN THE GROUND THAT FORMS ROCKS.

HOW A QUARTZ WATCH WORKS

hour hand

minute hand

battery

quartz oscillator

motor

circuit board

19

ATOMIC CLOCKS

The best machines used to keep time today are called atomic clocks. Atomic clocks measure the movement of tiny atoms to tell time. Most clocks use an **isotope** named cesium 133. Clocks using cesium 133 measure the number of times a cesium atom moves around in an excited state, or frequency.

Some scientists are working with **lasers** to make something called an **optical** clock. This clock measures 430 trillion light waves per second and is even more accurate than an atomic clock.

OOPS!

In 1967, scientists decided 1 second was the length of time it takes a cesium atom to move 9,192,631,770 times between two specific energy levels.

MEASURING THE MOVEMENT OF TINY ATOMS IS THE MOST ACCURATE WAY SCIENTISTS HAVE MEASURED TIME.

21

GLOSSARY

accurate: free from mistakes

archaeologist: a scientist who studies past human life and activities

crosspiece: something placed so as to cross something else

cycle: a period of time marked by certain events

gravity: the force that pulls objects toward Earth's center

isotope: one of two or more forms of atoms in the same element

laser: a narrow beam of light energy

mechanical: having to do with machines

optical: relating to vision

oscillator: a device that creates an electric charge

FOR MORE INFORMATION

BOOKS

Somervill, Barbara A. *The History of the Clock*. Chanhassen, MN: The Child's World, 2005.

Spilsbury, Richard, and Louise Spilbury. *The Clock*. Chicago, IL: Heinemann, 2012.

Woods, Michael, and Mary B. Woods. *Ancient Computing Technology: From Abacuses to Water Clocks*. Minneapolis, MN: Twenty-First Century Books, 2011.

WEBSITES

Building a Water Clock
sciencenetlinks.com/lessons/building-a-water-clock/
Build your own water clock with the help of this great site.

Official US Time
time.gov
Find out the official time in different parts of the United States and where the sun is shining on Earth.

INDEX